THE

J.E.S.U.S.

CHALLENGE

THE J.E.S.U.S. CHALLENGE

A 31-Day Prayer Journal to Grow
Your Relationship with God

MADELINE GRACE

a division of Baker Publishing Group
Grand Rapids, Michigan

Published by Revell
a division of Baker Publishing Group
Grand Rapids, Michigan
RevellBooks.com

Printed in the United States of America

Library of Congress Cataloging-in-Publication Data
Names: Grace, Madeline, 1994- author.
Title: The Jesus challenge : a 31-day prayer journal to grow your relationship with God / Madeline Grace.
Description: Grand Rapids, Michigan : Revell, a division of Baker Publishing Group, [2025]
Identifiers: LCCN 2024057073 | ISBN 9780800746933 (paperback) | ISBN 9781493450602 (ebook)
Subjects: LCSH: Bible—Quotations. | Spiritual journals—Authorship.
Classification: LCC BS2310 .G63 2025 | DDC 242/.2—dc23/eng/20250103
LC record available at https://lccn.loc.gov/2024057073

Cover design by Laura Powell

Baker Publishing Group publications use paper produced from sustainable forestry practices and postconsumer waste whenever possible.

25 26 27 28 29 30 31 7 6 5 4 3

Contents

Introduction

Hi friend!

Can I just start off by saying I am so unbelievably excited for you? All God needs and wants is a willing heart, and the fact that you want to do this challenge is proof of exactly that! I just know God is going to do amazing things during your time with Him. I discovered Jesus was real through a similar challenge over a decade ago when I journaled to Him like I would a friend, and my life has never been the same. The freedom, joy, purpose, confidence, provision, protection, and friendship He's given me have been endless, and if He's done it for me, He can do it for you. I'm praying that this challenge brings you everything your heart needs, but most importantly that it opens your eyes to a friendship that will change your life forever. My biggest piece of advice: be as unfiltered as possible with Him. The more you give God your heart, your WHOLE heart—the good, the bad, and the ugly—the more He can wrap His love around it. His love is the same power that raised Jesus from the dead, which means He has power over every evil thing, so nothing is off-limits. Get specific, dream big then dream a little more, get angry if you need to, tell Him about your unbelief, ask Him questions when you have them. God isn't intimidated by your feelings even when they include doubting who He is. When you give God your doubt, that's you inviting Him to tell you what's true and what's not. That's you giving Him an opportunity to prove your doubt wrong. His Word says ask and you will receive, so get specific. I'm talking, "Lord, I want to be and do ________ by this time next year" specific. You ready? Let's do this thang. @God, I'll let You take it from here.

How to Use the J.E.S.U.S. Challenge Method

The J.E.S.U.S. Challenge is a simple method that helps you develop a relationship with God on a daily basis. Not only does it help simplify getting to know God, but it helps you learn how to hear from God, read the Bible, and get to know who He created you to be. When it comes to developing a relationship with God, we sometimes make it more complicated than it needs to be, and it's easy to feel overwhelmed with where to start or how to do it. My goal is to help simplify it so you feel capable to develop and maintain your relationship with God long-term. The goal is to make it a lifestyle!

So here's the deal . . . the challenge is an acronym.

J—Journal

E—Experience

S—Study

U—Understand

S—Speak

Each day you will use this acronym during your time with God. The best way to develop long-term habits is to start small. I encourage you to dedicate at least thirty minutes to this every day. For reference, I usually spend about one hour, but don't put any pressure on yourself! The goal is progress, not perfection.

I recommend you schedule this time every day like you would for any class or appointment. All you need is a journal (check!), a Bible, and a pen.

Now, you might be wondering, "What do I do with each letter?" I'm so glad you asked:

J—Journal

Journal to God. Use this space to tell God what's on your heart and talk to Him like you would a friend. I start my entries with "Hi Jesus." I tell Him about the things I'm worried about, my prayer requests, what I want to see change in my life, what I'm struggling with, my dreams, and so on. The more we let God in on how we're thinking and feeling, the more we'll allow Him to help us with those things and the less alone we'll feel in accomplishing them. Nothing is off-limits. Our thoughts are safest with Him.

E—Experience

Experience God's presence. Simply sit in God's presence and experience His love. I encourage you to put on some worship music. The QR code to the right will take you to the playlist I use. Take some time to listen and worship. We just gave God our heart in the journaling portion; now it's time for God to show us His. This page is a place for you to write down what you think God is saying to you. So often we have a lot to say to God and don't spend enough time listening to what God is saying to us. This is a time to experience His power, which will not only equip us to get all our needs met by Him but help us go deeper in our relationship with Him. When we sit and experience God's presence, the enemy has no choice but to leave. The key is to let God love you as you are. The more you allow His love to filter into your heart, the more you'll start to transform from the inside out.

itsmadelinegrace/learn-more

S—Study

Study the daily verse. You can either follow one of the monthly plans I've provided for each verse of the day (you can find these starting on page 207) or you can choose your own verse each day. I encourage you to write down the verse, say it out loud, and then take some time to memorize it. There is so much power in memorizing Scripture because we can use it as a weapon when the enemy tries to whisper lies in our ears. It reminds us of what God says when we forget His promises. Remember, God's truth has power over every evil thing.

U—Understand

Understand the daily verse. Now it's time to try to understand the verse of the day by asking yourself the three questions below. It's easy for the Bible to feel like just a bunch of words until we're intentional about understanding it and applying it to our lives. I encourage you to pray before this portion and ask the Holy Spirit to help you understand anything He wants you to know.

Example prayer:

Holy Spirit, I pray You would help me understand the verse of the day in a personal way. I pray You would speak to me and help me pick up anything You're trying to say. You created my brain, Lord, so I trust that if You want me to learn from Your Word, You will help simplify it for me and it will click when You want it to. I pray I learn more about You, myself, and how to practically apply this verse to my life today. Amen.

Ask yourself these three questions:

- What does this verse teach me about God?
- What does this verse teach me about myself?
- How can I apply this verse to my life today?

S—Speak

Say a prayer. This page is for you to gather everything you've experienced in the other four sections and put it into a prayer. I encourage you to use your words to declare the verse of the day over your life, add prayer requests, and stand in agreement with God's truth. The power of life and death is in your tongue. When we use our words to speak God's truth over our life, we can stand confidently in the authority we have in Jesus.

DATE:

J—JOURNAL TO JESUS

Tell God what's on your heart. Talk to Him like you would a friend. You can use the journal prompts in the back of the book if you need a little help to start.

E—EXPERIENCE HIS PRESENCE

Worship, listen, and sit in His presence. Let Him love you as you are, and write down anything you think He might be saying.

S—STUDY THE VERSE

Write down the verse of the day, say it out loud, and try to memorize it.

U—UNDERSTAND THE VERSE

Take a moment to pray and ask the Holy Spirit to help you understand the verse.

Ask yourself these three questions:

- What does this verse teach you about God?

- What does this verse teach you about yourself?

- How can you apply this verse to your life?

S—SAY A PRAYER

Summarize your time and put it into a prayer. Speak the verse of the day over your life, add your prayer requests, and add any more thoughts to your conversation with God.

DATE:

J—JOURNAL TO JESUS

Tell God what's on your heart. Talk to Him like you would a friend. You can use the journal prompts in the back of the book if you need a little help to start.

E—EXPERIENCE HIS PRESENCE

Worship, listen, and sit in His presence. Let Him love you as you are, and write down anything you think He might be saying.

S—STUDY THE VERSE

Write down the verse of the day, say it out loud, and try to memorize it.

U—UNDERSTAND THE VERSE

Take a moment to pray and ask the Holy Spirit to help you understand the verse.

Ask yourself these three questions:

- What does this verse teach you about God?

- What does this verse teach you about yourself?

- How can you apply this verse to your life?

S—SAY A PRAYER

Summarize your time and put it into a prayer. Speak the verse of the day over your life, add your prayer requests, and add any more thoughts to your conversation with God.

DATE:

J—JOURNAL TO JESUS

Tell God what's on your heart. Talk to Him like you would a friend. You can use the journal prompts in the back of the book if you need a little help to start.

E—EXPERIENCE HIS PRESENCE

Worship, listen, and sit in His presence. Let Him love you as you are, and write down anything you think He might be saying.

S—STUDY THE VERSE

Write down the verse of the day, say it out loud, and try to memorize it.

U—UNDERSTAND THE VERSE

Take a moment to pray and ask the Holy Spirit to help you understand the verse.

Ask yourself these three questions:

- What does this verse teach you about God?

- What does this verse teach you about yourself?

- How can you apply this verse to your life?

S—SAY A PRAYER

Summarize your time and put it into a prayer. Speak the verse of the day over your life, add your prayer requests, and add any more thoughts to your conversation with God.

DATE:

J—JOURNAL TO JESUS

Tell God what's on your heart. Talk to Him like you would a friend. You can use the journal prompts in the back of the book if you need a little help to start.

E—EXPERIENCE HIS PRESENCE

Worship, listen, and sit in His presence. Let Him love you as you are, and write down anything you think He might be saying.

S—STUDY THE VERSE

Write down the verse of the day, say it out loud, and try to memorize it.

U—UNDERSTAND THE VERSE

Take a moment to pray and ask the Holy Spirit to help you understand the verse.

Ask yourself these three questions:

- What does this verse teach you about God?

- What does this verse teach you about yourself?

- How can you apply this verse to your life?

S—SAY A PRAYER

Summarize your time and put it into a prayer. Speak the verse of the day over your life, add your prayer requests, and add any more thoughts to your conversation with God.

DATE:

J—JOURNAL TO JESUS

Tell God what's on your heart. Talk to Him like you would a friend. You can use the journal prompts in the back of the book if you need a little help to start.

E—EXPERIENCE HIS PRESENCE

Worship, listen, and sit in His presence. Let Him love you as you are, and write down anything you think He might be saying.

S—STUDY THE VERSE

Write down the verse of the day, say it out loud, and try to memorize it.

U—UNDERSTAND THE VERSE

Take a moment to pray and ask the Holy Spirit to help you understand the verse.

Ask yourself these three questions:

- What does this verse teach you about God?

- What does this verse teach you about yourself?

- How can you apply this verse to your life?

S—SAY A PRAYER

Summarize your time and put it into a prayer. Speak the verse of the day over your life, add your prayer requests, and add any more thoughts to your conversation with God.

DATE:

J—JOURNAL TO JESUS

Tell God what's on your heart. Talk to Him like you would a friend. You can use the journal prompts in the back of the book if you need a little help to start.

E—EXPERIENCE HIS PRESENCE

Worship, listen, and sit in His presence. Let Him love you as you are, and write down anything you think He might be saying.

S—STUDY THE VERSE

Write down the verse of the day, say it out loud, and try to memorize it.

U—UNDERSTAND THE VERSE

Take a moment to pray and ask the Holy Spirit to help you understand the verse.

Ask yourself these three questions:

- What does this verse teach you about God?

- What does this verse teach you about yourself?

- How can you apply this verse to your life?

S—SAY A PRAYER

Summarize your time and put it into a prayer. Speak the verse of the day over your life, add your prayer requests, and add any more thoughts to your conversation with God.

DATE:

J—JOURNAL TO JESUS

Tell God what's on your heart. Talk to Him like you would a friend. You can use the journal prompts in the back of the book if you need a little help to start.

E—EXPERIENCE HIS PRESENCE

Worship, listen, and sit in His presence. Let Him love you as you are, and write down anything you think He might be saying.

S—STUDY THE VERSE

Write down the verse of the day, say it out loud, and try to memorize it.

U—UNDERSTAND THE VERSE

Take a moment to pray and ask the Holy Spirit to help you understand the verse.

Ask yourself these three questions:

- What does this verse teach you about God?

- What does this verse teach you about yourself?

- How can you apply this verse to your life?

S—SAY A PRAYER

Summarize your time and put it into a prayer. Speak the verse of the day over your life, add your prayer requests, and add any more thoughts to your conversation with God.

DATE:

J—JOURNAL TO JESUS

Tell God what's on your heart. Talk to Him like you would a friend. You can use the journal prompts in the back of the book if you need a little help to start.

E—EXPERIENCE HIS PRESENCE

Worship, listen, and sit in His presence. Let Him love you as you are, and write down anything you think He might be saying.

S—STUDY THE VERSE

Write down the verse of the day, say it out loud, and try to memorize it.

U—UNDERSTAND THE VERSE

Take a moment to pray and ask the Holy Spirit to help you understand the verse.

Ask yourself these three questions:

- What does this verse teach you about God?

- What does this verse teach you about yourself?

- How can you apply this verse to your life?

S—SAY A PRAYER

Summarize your time and put it into a prayer. Speak the verse of the day over your life, add your prayer requests, and add any more thoughts to your conversation with God.

DATE:

J—JOURNAL TO JESUS

Tell God what's on your heart. Talk to Him like you would a friend. You can use the journal prompts in the back of the book if you need a little help to start.

E—EXPERIENCE HIS PRESENCE

Worship, listen, and sit in His presence. Let Him love you as you are, and write down anything you think He might be saying.

S—STUDY THE VERSE

Write down the verse of the day, say it out loud, and try to memorize it.

U—UNDERSTAND THE VERSE

Take a moment to pray and ask the Holy Spirit to help you understand the verse.

Ask yourself these three questions:

- What does this verse teach you about God?

- What does this verse teach you about yourself?

- How can you apply this verse to your life?

S—SAY A PRAYER

Summarize your time and put it into a prayer. Speak the verse of the day over your life, add your prayer requests, and add any more thoughts to your conversation with God.

DATE:

J—JOURNAL TO JESUS

Tell God what's on your heart. Talk to Him like you would a friend. You can use the journal prompts in the back of the book if you need a little help to start.

E—EXPERIENCE HIS PRESENCE

Worship, listen, and sit in His presence. Let Him love you as you are, and write down anything you think He might be saying.

S—STUDY THE VERSE

Write down the verse of the day, say it out loud, and try to memorize it.

U—UNDERSTAND THE VERSE

Take a moment to pray and ask the Holy Spirit to help you understand the verse.

Ask yourself these three questions:

- What does this verse teach you about God?

- What does this verse teach you about yourself?

- How can you apply this verse to your life?

S—SAY A PRAYER

Summarize your time and put it into a prayer. Speak the verse of the day over your life, add your prayer requests, and add any more thoughts to your conversation with God.

DATE:

J—JOURNAL TO JESUS

Tell God what's on your heart. Talk to Him like you would a friend. You can use the journal prompts in the back of the book if you need a little help to start.

E—EXPERIENCE HIS PRESENCE

Worship, listen, and sit in His presence. Let Him love you as you are, and write down anything you think He might be saying.

S—STUDY THE VERSE

Write down the verse of the day, say it out loud, and try to memorize it.

U—UNDERSTAND THE VERSE

Take a moment to pray and ask the Holy Spirit to help you understand the verse.

Ask yourself these three questions:

- What does this verse teach you about God?

- What does this verse teach you about yourself?

- How can you apply this verse to your life?

S—SAY A PRAYER

Summarize your time and put it into a prayer. Speak the verse of the day over your life, add your prayer requests, and add any more thoughts to your conversation with God.

DATE:

J—JOURNAL TO JESUS

Tell God what's on your heart. Talk to Him like you would a friend. You can use the journal prompts in the back of the book if you need a little help to start.

E—EXPERIENCE HIS PRESENCE

Worship, listen, and sit in His presence. Let Him love you as you are, and write down anything you think He might be saying.

S—STUDY THE VERSE

Write down the verse of the day, say it out loud, and try to memorize it.

U—UNDERSTAND THE VERSE

Take a moment to pray and ask the Holy Spirit to help you understand the verse.

Ask yourself these three questions:

- What does this verse teach you about God?

- What does this verse teach you about yourself?

- How can you apply this verse to your life?

S—SAY A PRAYER

Summarize your time and put it into a prayer. Speak the verse of the day over your life, add your prayer requests, and add any more thoughts to your conversation with God.

DATE:

J—JOURNAL TO JESUS

Tell God what's on your heart. Talk to Him like you would a friend. You can use the journal prompts in the back of the book if you need a little help to start.

E—EXPERIENCE HIS PRESENCE

Worship, listen, and sit in His presence. Let Him love you as you are, and write down anything you think He might be saying.

S—STUDY THE VERSE

Write down the verse of the day, say it out loud, and try to memorize it.

U—UNDERSTAND THE VERSE

Take a moment to pray and ask the Holy Spirit to help you understand the verse.

Ask yourself these three questions:

- What does this verse teach you about God?

- What does this verse teach you about yourself?

- How can you apply this verse to your life?

S—SAY A PRAYER

Summarize your time and put it into a prayer. Speak the verse of the day over your life, add your prayer requests, and add any more thoughts to your conversation with God.

DATE:

J—JOURNAL TO JESUS

Tell God what's on your heart. Talk to Him like you would a friend. You can use the journal prompts in the back of the book if you need a little help to start.

E—EXPERIENCE HIS PRESENCE

Worship, listen, and sit in His presence. Let Him love you as you are, and write down anything you think He might be saying.

S—STUDY THE VERSE

Write down the verse of the day, say it out loud, and try to memorize it.

U—UNDERSTAND THE VERSE

Take a moment to pray and ask the Holy Spirit to help you understand the verse.

Ask yourself these three questions:

- What does this verse teach you about God?

- What does this verse teach you about yourself?

- How can you apply this verse to your life?

S—SAY A PRAYER

Summarize your time and put it into a prayer. Speak the verse of the day over your life, add your prayer requests, and add any more thoughts to your conversation with God.

DATE:

J—JOURNAL TO JESUS

Tell God what's on your heart. Talk to Him like you would a friend. You can use the journal prompts in the back of the book if you need a little help to start.

E—EXPERIENCE HIS PRESENCE

Worship, listen, and sit in His presence. Let Him love you as you are, and write down anything you think He might be saying.

S—STUDY THE VERSE

Write down the verse of the day, say it out loud, and try to memorize it.

U—UNDERSTAND THE VERSE

Take a moment to pray and ask the Holy Spirit to help you understand the verse.

Ask yourself these three questions:

- What does this verse teach you about God?

- What does this verse teach you about yourself?

- How can you apply this verse to your life?

S—SAY A PRAYER

Summarize your time and put it into a prayer. Speak the verse of the day over your life, add your prayer requests, and add any more thoughts to your conversation with God.

DATE:

J—JOURNAL TO JESUS

Tell God what's on your heart. Talk to Him like you would a friend. You can use the journal prompts in the back of the book if you need a little help to start.

E—EXPERIENCE HIS PRESENCE

Worship, listen, and sit in His presence. Let Him love you as you are, and write down anything you think He might be saying.

S—STUDY THE VERSE

Write down the verse of the day, say it out loud, and try to memorize it.

U—UNDERSTAND THE VERSE

Take a moment to pray and ask the Holy Spirit to help you understand the verse.

Ask yourself these three questions:

- What does this verse teach you about God?

- What does this verse teach you about yourself?

- How can you apply this verse to your life?

S—SAY A PRAYER

Summarize your time and put it into a prayer. Speak the verse of the day over your life, add your prayer requests, and add any more thoughts to your conversation with God.

DATE:

J—JOURNAL TO JESUS

Tell God what's on your heart. Talk to Him like you would a friend. You can use the journal prompts in the back of the book if you need a little help to start.

E—EXPERIENCE HIS PRESENCE

Worship, listen, and sit in His presence. Let Him love you as you are, and write down anything you think He might be saying.

S—STUDY THE VERSE

Write down the verse of the day, say it out loud, and try to memorize it.

U—UNDERSTAND THE VERSE

Take a moment to pray and ask the Holy Spirit to help you understand the verse.

Ask yourself these three questions:

- What does this verse teach you about God?

- What does this verse teach you about yourself?

- How can you apply this verse to your life?

S—SAY A PRAYER

Summarize your time and put it into a prayer. Speak the verse of the day over your life, add your prayer requests, and add any more thoughts to your conversation with God.

DATE:

J—JOURNAL TO JESUS

Tell God what's on your heart. Talk to Him like you would a friend. You can use the journal prompts in the back of the book if you need a little help to start.

E—EXPERIENCE HIS PRESENCE

Worship, listen, and sit in His presence. Let Him love you as you are, and write down anything you think He might be saying.

S—STUDY THE VERSE

Write down the verse of the day, say it out loud, and try to memorize it.

U—UNDERSTAND THE VERSE

Take a moment to pray and ask the Holy Spirit to help you understand the verse.

Ask yourself these three questions:

- What does this verse teach you about God?

- What does this verse teach you about yourself?

- How can you apply this verse to your life?

S—SAY A PRAYER

Summarize your time and put it into a prayer. Speak the verse of the day over your life, add your prayer requests, and add any more thoughts to your conversation with God.

DATE:

J—JOURNAL TO JESUS

Tell God what's on your heart. Talk to Him like you would a friend. You can use the journal prompts in the back of the book if you need a little help to start.

E—EXPERIENCE HIS PRESENCE

Worship, listen, and sit in His presence. Let Him love you as you are, and write down anything you think He might be saying.

S—STUDY THE VERSE

Write down the verse of the day, say it out loud, and try to memorize it.

U—UNDERSTAND THE VERSE

Take a moment to pray and ask the Holy Spirit to help you understand the verse.

Ask yourself these three questions:

- What does this verse teach you about God?

- What does this verse teach you about yourself?

- How can you apply this verse to your life?

S—SAY A PRAYER

Summarize your time and put it into a prayer. Speak the verse of the day over your life, add your prayer requests, and add any more thoughts to your conversation with God.

DATE:

J—JOURNAL TO JESUS

Tell God what's on your heart. Talk to Him like you would a friend. You can use the journal prompts in the back of the book if you need a little help to start.

E—EXPERIENCE HIS PRESENCE

Worship, listen, and sit in His presence. Let Him love you as you are, and write down anything you think He might be saying.

S—STUDY THE VERSE

Write down the verse of the day, say it out loud, and try to memorize it.

U—UNDERSTAND THE VERSE

Take a moment to pray and ask the Holy Spirit to help you understand the verse.

Ask yourself these three questions:

- What does this verse teach you about God?

- What does this verse teach you about yourself?

- How can you apply this verse to your life?

S—SAY A PRAYER

Summarize your time and put it into a prayer. Speak the verse of the day over your life, add your prayer requests, and add any more thoughts to your conversation with God.

DATE:

J—JOURNAL TO JESUS

Tell God what's on your heart. Talk to Him like you would a friend. You can use the journal prompts in the back of the book if you need a little help to start.

E—EXPERIENCE HIS PRESENCE

Worship, listen, and sit in His presence. Let Him love you as you are, and write down anything you think He might be saying.

S—STUDY THE VERSE

Write down the verse of the day, say it out loud, and try to memorize it.

U—UNDERSTAND THE VERSE

Take a moment to pray and ask the Holy Spirit to help you understand the verse.

Ask yourself these three questions:

- What does this verse teach you about God?

- What does this verse teach you about yourself?

- How can you apply this verse to your life?

S—SAY A PRAYER

Summarize your time and put it into a prayer. Speak the verse of the day over your life, add your prayer requests, and add any more thoughts to your conversation with God.

DATE:

J—JOURNAL TO JESUS

Tell God what's on your heart. Talk to Him like you would a friend. You can use the journal prompts in the back of the book if you need a little help to start.

E—EXPERIENCE HIS PRESENCE

Worship, listen, and sit in His presence. Let Him love you as you are, and write down anything you think He might be saying.

S—STUDY THE VERSE

Write down the verse of the day, say it out loud, and try to memorize it.

U—UNDERSTAND THE VERSE

Take a moment to pray and ask the Holy Spirit to help you understand the verse.

Ask yourself these three questions:

- What does this verse teach you about God?

- What does this verse teach you about yourself?

- How can you apply this verse to your life?

S—SAY A PRAYER

Summarize your time and put it into a prayer. Speak the verse of the day over your life, add your prayer requests, and add any more thoughts to your conversation with God.

DATE:

J—JOURNAL TO JESUS

Tell God what's on your heart. Talk to Him like you would a friend. You can use the journal prompts in the back of the book if you need a little help to start.

E—EXPERIENCE HIS PRESENCE

Worship, listen, and sit in His presence. Let Him love you as you are, and write down anything you think He might be saying.

S—STUDY THE VERSE

Write down the verse of the day, say it out loud, and try to memorize it.

U—UNDERSTAND THE VERSE

Take a moment to pray and ask the Holy Spirit to help you understand the verse.

Ask yourself these three questions:

- What does this verse teach you about God?

- What does this verse teach you about yourself?

- How can you apply this verse to your life?

S—SAY A PRAYER

Summarize your time and put it into a prayer. Speak the verse of the day over your life, add your prayer requests, and add any more thoughts to your conversation with God.

DATE:

J—JOURNAL TO JESUS

Tell God what's on your heart. Talk to Him like you would a friend. You can use the journal prompts in the back of the book if you need a little help to start.

E—EXPERIENCE HIS PRESENCE

Worship, listen, and sit in His presence. Let Him love you as you are, and write down anything you think He might be saying.

S—STUDY THE VERSE

Write down the verse of the day, say it out loud, and try to memorize it.

U—UNDERSTAND THE VERSE

Take a moment to pray and ask the Holy Spirit to help you understand the verse.

Ask yourself these three questions:

- What does this verse teach you about God?

- What does this verse teach you about yourself?

- How can you apply this verse to your life?

S—SAY A PRAYER

Summarize your time and put it into a prayer. Speak the verse of the day over your life, add your prayer requests, and add any more thoughts to your conversation with God.

DATE:

J—JOURNAL TO JESUS

Tell God what's on your heart. Talk to Him like you would a friend. You can use the journal prompts in the back of the book if you need a little help to start.

E—EXPERIENCE HIS PRESENCE

Worship, listen, and sit in His presence. Let Him love you as you are, and write down anything you think He might be saying.

S—STUDY THE VERSE

Write down the verse of the day, say it out loud, and try to memorize it.

U—UNDERSTAND THE VERSE

Take a moment to pray and ask the Holy Spirit to help you understand the verse.

Ask yourself these three questions:

- What does this verse teach you about God?

- What does this verse teach you about yourself?

- How can you apply this verse to your life?

S—SAY A PRAYER

Summarize your time and put it into a prayer. Speak the verse of the day over your life, add your prayer requests, and add any more thoughts to your conversation with God.

DATE:

J—JOURNAL TO JESUS

Tell God what's on your heart. Talk to Him like you would a friend. You can use the journal prompts in the back of the book if you need a little help to start.

E—EXPERIENCE HIS PRESENCE

Worship, listen, and sit in His presence. Let Him love you as you are, and write down anything you think He might be saying.

S—STUDY THE VERSE

Write down the verse of the day, say it out loud, and try to memorize it.

U—UNDERSTAND THE VERSE

Take a moment to pray and ask the Holy Spirit to help you understand the verse.

Ask yourself these three questions:

- What does this verse teach you about God?

- What does this verse teach you about yourself?

- How can you apply this verse to your life?

S—SAY A PRAYER

Summarize your time and put it into a prayer. Speak the verse of the day over your life, add your prayer requests, and add any more thoughts to your conversation with God.

DATE:

J—JOURNAL TO JESUS

Tell God what's on your heart. Talk to Him like you would a friend. You can use the journal prompts in the back of the book if you need a little help to start.

E—EXPERIENCE HIS PRESENCE

Worship, listen, and sit in His presence. Let Him love you as you are, and write down anything you think He might be saying.

S—STUDY THE VERSE

Write down the verse of the day, say it out loud, and try to memorize it.

U—UNDERSTAND THE VERSE

Take a moment to pray and ask the Holy Spirit to help you understand the verse.

Ask yourself these three questions:

- What does this verse teach you about God?

- What does this verse teach you about yourself?

- How can you apply this verse to your life?

S—SAY A PRAYER

Summarize your time and put it into a prayer. Speak the verse of the day over your life, add your prayer requests, and add any more thoughts to your conversation with God.

DATE:

J—JOURNAL TO JESUS

Tell God what's on your heart. Talk to Him like you would a friend. You can use the journal prompts in the back of the book if you need a little help to start.

E—EXPERIENCE HIS PRESENCE

Worship, listen, and sit in His presence. Let Him love you as you are, and write down anything you think He might be saying.

S—STUDY THE VERSE

Write down the verse of the day, say it out loud, and try to memorize it.

U—UNDERSTAND THE VERSE

Take a moment to pray and ask the Holy Spirit to help you understand the verse.

Ask yourself these three questions:

- What does this verse teach you about God?

- What does this verse teach you about yourself?

- How can you apply this verse to your life?

S—SAY A PRAYER

Summarize your time and put it into a prayer. Speak the verse of the day over your life, add your prayer requests, and add any more thoughts to your conversation with God.

DATE:

J—JOURNAL TO JESUS

Tell God what's on your heart. Talk to Him like you would a friend. You can use the journal prompts in the back of the book if you need a little help to start.

E—EXPERIENCE HIS PRESENCE

Worship, listen, and sit in His presence. Let Him love you as you are, and write down anything you think He might be saying.

S—STUDY THE VERSE

Write down the verse of the day, say it out loud, and try to memorize it.

U—UNDERSTAND THE VERSE

Take a moment to pray and ask the Holy Spirit to help you understand the verse.

Ask yourself these three questions:

- What does this verse teach you about God?

- What does this verse teach you about yourself?

- How can you apply this verse to your life?

S—SAY A PRAYER

Summarize your time and put it into a prayer. Speak the verse of the day over your life, add your prayer requests, and add any more thoughts to your conversation with God.

DATE:

J—JOURNAL TO JESUS

Tell God what's on your heart. Talk to Him like you would a friend. You can use the journal prompts in the back of the book if you need a little help to start.

E—EXPERIENCE HIS PRESENCE

Worship, listen, and sit in His presence. Let Him love you as you are, and write down anything you think He might be saying.

S—STUDY THE VERSE

Write down the verse of the day, say it out loud, and try to memorize it.

U—UNDERSTAND THE VERSE

Take a moment to pray and ask the Holy Spirit to help you understand the verse.

Ask yourself these three questions:

- What does this verse teach you about God?

- What does this verse teach you about yourself?

- How can you apply this verse to your life?

S—SAY A PRAYER

Summarize your time and put it into a prayer. Speak the verse of the day over your life, add your prayer requests, and add any more thoughts to your conversation with God.

DATE:

J—JOURNAL TO JESUS

Tell God what's on your heart. Talk to Him like you would a friend. You can use the journal prompts in the back of the book if you need a little help to start.

E—EXPERIENCE HIS PRESENCE

Worship, listen, and sit in His presence. Let Him love you as you are, and write down anything you think He might be saying.

S—STUDY THE VERSE

Write down the verse of the day, say it out loud, and try to memorize it.

U—UNDERSTAND THE VERSE

Take a moment to pray and ask the Holy Spirit to help you understand the verse.

Ask yourself these three questions:

- What does this verse teach you about God?

- What does this verse teach you about yourself?

- How can you apply this verse to your life?

S—SAY A PRAYER

Summarize your time and put it into a prayer. Speak the verse of the day over your life, add your prayer requests, and add any more thoughts to your conversation with God.

CLOSING NOTE

If you've made it this far, I think congratulations are in order! You spent the last thirty-one days prioritizing your relationship with God. I hope this challenge helped you feel capable of developing a relationship with God. I hope it helped you hear and see Him in a new way. I hope it motivates you to continue, and I hope doing life with Him daily becomes your new normal. I'm so proud of you! Thank you for trusting me to lead you. You're officially a part of the J.E.S.U.S. Challenge fam! I can imagine that God has the biggest smile on His face. If this challenge blessed you, I encourage you to keep going for another thirty-one days.

Also, if you have a testimony from your experience, I would love to hear about it!

Please email me at MadelineGraceTrammell@gmail.com.

God bless you! <3

xx,
Madeline Grace

Journal Prompts

Journaling helps us be intentional with our thinking and helps us gain clarity about ourselves. The best way to gain clarity is to figure out what's going on in our thoughts, and we do this by asking ourselves questions. It's the simple questions that we usually don't think we need to answer that are actually the most important. So often we don't know basic things about ourselves because we never ask ourselves those simple questions that get us to really think.

These questions will help you get to the root issues of your problems and connect the dots in your life. I'm a firm believer in journaling because it helps you figure out right where you're at. There's no such thing as saying the wrong thing. This is a time for you to freely process with God. Sometimes we don't know what we believe or are functioning in until we ask ourselves questions. Once you get more connected to how you think and feel, you're going to better understand where you need to grow, and once you know where you need to grow, you're going to gain vision for where you want to go in life.

If we know where we're at and what we think about in certain areas in our life, then we know what to pray for, and that's when everything changes. The Bible says, "Ask and it will be given to you" (Matt. 7:7). The more specific we get in our prayer life, the more specifically God shows up.

These questions will build . . .

Vision for your relationship with God

Vision for who you want to be

Vision for what you want to do

Vision for the friends you want

Vision for your current/future family

Vision for your dreams

Vision for your relationships

Remember—God is doing this with you! I would recommend praying before answering each question.

If you pair these questions with intentional prayer and ask God to help you process them, I believe you're going to see and feel a lot of transformation in yourself.

Example prayer:

Lord, help me to answer this to the best of my ability. Help me to be as honest as possible so that I can use this question to get to know myself better and create the vision You have for my future. Amen.

The goal here is to help you get reconnected to your heart and to feel empowered to become the person God created you to be. The more connected you are to your heart, the more naturally journaling will come.

Prompts

GOD

1. Who is God to you?
2. How would you describe God to a friend who doesn't know Him?
3. What does God's love look like to you?
4. How has God changed your life?
5. Are there areas of your life where you've had doubts about God? Why?
6. What prayers has God answered in your life?

7. Why do you believe in God?
8. Where do you want your relationship with God to grow?
9. When do you feel the most loved by God?
10. How does God correct you?
11. How do you think God sees you?
12. When do you feel the most connected to God? What makes you feel disconnected?
13. When do you think God is most proud of you?
14. What does spending time with God look like to you?
15. In what ways do people experience God through you?
16. What areas of your life do you struggle to trust God in?
17. What do you think God created you for?
18. What do you want your relationship with God to look like this year?

SELF

1. Who are you to you?
2. How do you think others see you?
3. How do you wish others saw you?
4. What stresses you out, and how do you cope?
5. What do you think your God-given gifts are?
6. What do you enjoy doing?
7. What are your core values (e.g., love, courage, honesty, authenticity)?
8. What are you afraid of?
9. What areas of your life do you feel the most judged in?
10. How would you describe your childhood?
11. How has your childhood affected who you are today?
12. What are your insecurities?
13. What do you love about yourself?
14. What areas of your life do you want to see growth in?
15. What do you do when you feel overwhelmed?

16. How do you process pain?
17. What do boundaries look like to you?
18. What is most important to you?
19. What are your nonnegotiables in your life?
20. Who do you trust the most in your life and why?
21. What do you want your life to look like a year from now?
22. What type of person do you want to become (e.g., confident, decisive, bold, fearless in communication, patient, etc.)?

FAMILY

1. How do you view your family?
2. How would your family describe you?
3. In what ways does your family make you feel safe? Unsafe?
4. What generational curses are/were on your family? How do they / have they manifested in your life?
5. What kind of people would you like to see your family become?
6. How was/is your relationship with your mom or mother figure? How has that affected who you are today? Positively and negatively?
7. How was/is your relationship with your dad or father figure? How has that affected who you are today? Positively and negatively?
8. What role do you play in your family? What do you like or dislike about that?
9. What parts of you do you wish your family knew?
10. What do you love about your family?
11. What character qualities have you learned from your family?
12. How do you handle conflict in your family?
13. What does communication look like in your family?
14. What do you admire about your friends' families?
15. When do you feel the most loved by your family?
16. When do you feel the most disconnected from your family?

17. What aspects of your family do you wish to bring into your current/future family? What aspects do you wish to leave behind?
18. What do you want your relationship with your family to look like next year?

FRIENDS

1. What are your friends like?
2. How do your friends challenge and inspire you?
3. How do your friends make you feel?
4. How do you think your friends view you?
5. How do you wish your friends viewed you?
6. Who are the friends who tell you the truth even when you don't want to hear it? How do you respond in those moments?
7. After hanging out with your friends, do you leave loving who you are? Or do you overthink about the things you wish you were?
8. What do you value in friendship?
9. Who are the friends you want to be more like? What is it about them that makes you want to be like them?
10. Who are the friends who celebrate who you are? How do they celebrate you?
11. Who are the friends who bring you closer to God? What does that look like?
12. What value do your friends bring to your life? Are they givers or takers? What role do you play?

DREAMS/GOALS

1. What do you think your purpose is? Why do you think God created you?
2. What makes you unique?
3. If money didn't matter, what would you do?
4. What comes naturally to you?
5. What makes you feel alive?

6. What are the things that people tell you you're good at?
7. How do people explain how you make them feel?
8. Is there anything you want to learn how to do? If so, why haven't you started yet?
9. Do you tell God about your dreams? If not, why? If you do, what are they?
10. What is your definition of success?
11. What do you want to see come to pass in this next year?

Guided Monthly Bible Challenges

Follow the QR code below and use discount code TJCJOURNAL for free access to the corresponding video collection for each book.

itsmadelinegrace.com/learn-more

MATTHEW

WEEK 1

- ☐ Matthew 5:3
- ☐ Matthew 6:33
- ☐ Matthew 7:7–8
- ☐ Matthew 11:28
- ☐ Matthew 16:25
- ☐ Matthew 22:37–39
- ☐ Matthew 26:41

WEEK 2

- ☐ Matthew 4:1
- ☐ Matthew 6:24
- ☐ Matthew 6:14–15
- ☐ Matthew 10:19–20
- ☐ Matthew 7:1–2
- ☐ Matthew 5:44
- ☐ Matthew 6:34

WEEK 3

- ☐ Matthew 7:24–25
- ☐ Matthew 9:13
- ☐ Matthew 7:6
- ☐ Matthew 3:2
- ☐ Matthew 25:21
- ☐ Matthew 14:29–31
- ☐ Matthew 9:22

WEEK 4

- ☐ Matthew 5:37
- ☐ Matthew 18:3–4
- ☐ Matthew 19:19
- ☐ Matthew 22:29
- ☐ Matthew 6:22
- ☐ Matthew 18:19–20
- ☐ Matthew 28:18–20

MARK

WEEK 1

- ☐ Mark 1:15
- ☐ Mark 8:34–35
- ☐ Mark 1:12–13
- ☐ Mark 12:29–31
- ☐ Mark 11:24–25
- ☐ Mark 9:23–24
- ☐ Mark 16:16

WEEK 2

- ☐ Mark 2:17
- ☐ Mark 4:22
- ☐ Mark 7:15
- ☐ Mark 4:24–25
- ☐ Mark 9:49–50
- ☐ Mark 10:14–15
- ☐ Mark 10:23–25

WEEK 3

- ☐ Mark 12:24
- ☐ Mark 13:11
- ☐ Mark 14:38
- ☐ Mark 13:13
- ☐ Mark 4:30–32
- ☐ Mark 2:2–5
- ☐ Mark 10:51–52

WEEK 4

- ☐ Mark 2:27–28
- ☐ Mark 2:19–20
- ☐ Mark 4:38–40
- ☐ Mark 4:3–9
- ☐ Mark 15:24–28
- ☐ Mark 14:36
- ☐ Mark 16:5–7

LUKE

WEEK 1

- ☐ Luke 15:24
- ☐ Luke 4:1–2
- ☐ Luke 5:31
- ☐ Luke 6:20–21
- ☐ Luke 6:46–48
- ☐ Luke 8:5–8
- ☐ Luke 9:23–24

WEEK 2

- ☐ Luke 10:18–19
- ☐ Luke 22:46
- ☐ Luke 11:9–10
- ☐ Luke 11:28
- ☐ Luke 11:34
- ☐ Luke 12:11–12
- ☐ Luke 12:25–26

WEEK 3

- ☐ Luke 12:31
- ☐ Luke 23:40–43
- ☐ Luke 14:11
- ☐ Luke 22:19–20
- ☐ Luke 1:30–35
- ☐ Luke 2:10–11
- ☐ Luke 16:10

JOHN

WEEK 1

- ☐ John 3:16
- ☐ John 1:12–13
- ☐ John 15:4
- ☐ John 13:35
- ☐ John 14:6–7
- ☐ John 16:12–13
- ☐ John 16:33

WEEK 2

- ☐ John 15:18
- ☐ John 2:24–25
- ☐ John 3:20–21
- ☐ John 10:4–5
- ☐ John 4:13–14
- ☐ John 5:39–42
- ☐ John 6:29

WEEK 3

- ☐ John 4:10
- ☐ John 16:7–8
- ☐ John 7:15–16
- ☐ John 8:7
- ☐ John 8:31–32
- ☐ John 9:3
- ☐ John 15:9–10

WEEK 4

- ☐ John 3:3
- ☐ John 10:10
- ☐ John 13:34
- ☐ John 14:15–17
- ☐ John 14:26
- ☐ John 4:34
- ☐ John 3:30

PSALMS

WEEK 1

- ☐ Psalm 23:1–4
- ☐ Psalm 103:12–14
- ☐ Psalm 66:18–20
- ☐ Psalm 111:10
- ☐ Psalm 37:4
- ☐ Psalm 139:23–24
- ☐ Psalm 55:22

WEEK 2

- ☐ Psalm 119:105
- ☐ Psalm 118:24
- ☐ Psalm 34:12–14
- ☐ Psalm 37:23
- ☐ Psalm 118:8
- ☐ Psalm 147:3
- ☐ Psalm 34:4–6

WEEK 3

- ☐ Psalm 27:1
- ☐ Psalm 34:8–10
- ☐ Psalm 46:10
- ☐ Psalm 139:16
- ☐ Psalm 119:9–11
- ☐ Psalm 1:1–4
- ☐ Psalm 9:1–2

WEEK 4

- ☐ Psalm 46:1
- ☐ Psalm 112:7
- ☐ Psalm 89:14
- ☐ Psalm 51:10
- ☐ Psalm 50:14
- ☐ Psalm 62:5–8
- ☐ Psalm 16:11

PROVERBS

WEEK 1

- ☐ Proverbs 9:10
- ☐ Proverbs 2:3–5
- ☐ Proverbs 3:5–6
- ☐ Proverbs 4:23
- ☐ Proverbs 3:11–12
- ☐ Proverbs 1:23
- ☐ Proverbs 3:21–24

WEEK 2

- ☐ Proverbs 11:2
- ☐ Proverbs 31:30
- ☐ Proverbs 12:12
- ☐ Proverbs 12:16
- ☐ Proverbs 13:12
- ☐ Proverbs 13:20
- ☐ Proverbs 14:9

WEEK 3

- ☐ Proverbs 14:30
- ☐ Proverbs 16:1
- ☐ Proverbs 26:4
- ☐ Proverbs 16:28
- ☐ Proverbs 16:2
- ☐ Proverbs 17:22
- ☐ Proverbs 19:2

WEEK 4

- ☐ Proverbs 17:3
- ☐ Proverbs 19:3
- ☐ Proverbs 19:8
- ☐ Proverbs 20:12
- ☐ Proverbs 19:19
- ☐ Proverbs 20:1
- ☐ Proverbs 20:24

WEEK 5

- ☐ Proverbs 20:27
- ☐ Proverbs 3:9–10
- ☐ Proverbs 22:6
- ☐ Proverbs 24:10
- ☐ Proverbs 10:19
- ☐ Proverbs 24:6
- ☐ Proverbs 21:30

ACTS

WEEK 1

- ☐ Acts 2:24
- ☐ Acts 4:12
- ☐ Acts 2:21
- ☐ Acts 2:38
- ☐ Acts 1:8
- ☐ Acts 5:32
- ☐ Acts 2:26

WEEK 2

- ☐ Acts 3:19–20
- ☐ Acts 9:31
- ☐ Acts 5:29
- ☐ Acts 17:24–25
- ☐ Acts 10:38
- ☐ Acts 14:21–22
- ☐ Acts 10:28

WEEK 3

- ☐ Acts 13:39
- ☐ Acts 17:27–28
- ☐ Acts 3:16
- ☐ Acts 13:22
- ☐ Acts 4:13
- ☐ Acts 17:11–12
- ☐ Acts 10:34–36

WEEK 4

- ☐ Acts 4:32
- ☐ Acts 17:30
- ☐ Acts 15:8–11
- ☐ Acts 14:10–11
- ☐ Acts 18:9
- ☐ Acts 2:42
- ☐ Acts 2:28

ROMANS

WEEK 1

- ☐ Romans 3:23–24
- ☐ Romans 10:9–10
- ☐ Romans 8:5–6
- ☐ Romans 12:2
- ☐ Romans 8:1–2
- ☐ Romans 12:3
- ☐ Romans 8:38–39

WEEK 2

- ☐ Romans 5:3–5
- ☐ Romans 12:9–10
- ☐ Romans 11:29
- ☐ Romans 5:18–19
- ☐ Romans 8:28
- ☐ Romans 10:13
- ☐ Romans 10:17

WEEK 3

- ☐ Romans 8:9
- ☐ Romans 6:1–4
- ☐ Romans 8:31
- ☐ Romans 15:4
- ☐ Romans 2:4
- ☐ Romans 10:14–15
- ☐ Romans 8:15–16

WEEK 4

- ☐ Romans 13:8
- ☐ Romans 3:27–28
- ☐ Romans 8:25
- ☐ Romans 1:21
- ☐ Romans 12:4–5
- ☐ Romans 3:3–4
- ☐ Romans 5:11

WEEK 5

- ☐ Romans 15:13
- ☐ Romans 6:16–17
- ☐ Romans 7:7
- ☐ Romans 7:14–17
- ☐ Romans 12:14–16
- ☐ Romans 12:12
- ☐ Romans 14:22–23

1 CORINTHIANS

WEEK 1

- ☐ 1 Corinthians 1:30–31
- ☐ 1 Corinthians 2:10–12
- ☐ 1 Corinthians 13:4–7
- ☐ 1 Corinthians 13:1–3
- ☐ 1 Corinthians 10:13
- ☐ 1 Corinthians 4:7
- ☐ 1 Corinthians 4:20

WEEK 2

- ☐ 1 Corinthians 3:1–3
- ☐ 1 Corinthians 6:18–20
- ☐ 1 Corinthians 6:12
- ☐ 1 Corinthians 2:13–15
- ☐ 1 Corinthians 15:21
- ☐ 1 Corinthians 11:23–25
- ☐ 1 Corinthians 7:32–35

WEEK 3

- ☐ 1 Corinthians 15:58
- ☐ 1 Corinthians 4:4–5
- ☐ 1 Corinthians 7:19
- ☐ 1 Corinthians 7:29–31
- ☐ 1 Corinthians 8:2–3
- ☐ 1 Corinthians 1:8–9
- ☐ 1 Corinthians 9:22–23

WEEK 4

- ☐ 1 Corinthians 15:2
- ☐ 1 Corinthians 10:21–22
- ☐ 1 Corinthians 12:4–6
- ☐ 1 Corinthians 15:33–34
- ☐ 1 Corinthians 15:10–11
- ☐ 1 Corinthians 13:13
- ☐ 1 Corinthians 16:13–14

GALATIANS

WEEK 1

- ☐ Galatians 1:4–5
- ☐ Galatians 2:16
- ☐ Galatians 3:26–27
- ☐ Galatians 4:6–7
- ☐ Galatians 2:20
- ☐ Galatians 5:16–18
- ☐ Galatians 5:22–23

WEEK 2

- ☐ Galatians 3:3
- ☐ Galatians 6:4–5
- ☐ Galatians 1:10
- ☐ Galatians 1:15–16
- ☐ Galatians 2:17–18
- ☐ Galatians 5:24–25
- ☐ Galatians 2:19

WEEK 3

- ☐ Galatians 6:9
- ☐ Galatians 5:19–21
- ☐ Galatians 6:1
- ☐ Galatians 6:7–8
- ☐ Galatians 5:7–8
- ☐ Galatians 6:14
- ☐ Galatians 5:13–14

WEEK 4

- ☐ Galatians 1:12
- ☐ Galatians 6:3
- ☐ Galatians 5:9–10
- ☐ Galatians 3:13
- ☐ Galatians 3:29
- ☐ Galatians 5:1
- ☐ Galatians 6:15–16

EPHESIANS

WEEK 1

- ☐ Ephesians 1:4–5
- ☐ Ephesians 1:7–8
- ☐ Ephesians 1:13–14
- ☐ Ephesians 2:4–6
- ☐ Ephesians 2:8–9
- ☐ Ephesians 2:18
- ☐ Ephesians 3:12

WEEK 2

- ☐ Ephesians 1:16–18
- ☐ Ephesians 3:17–19
- ☐ Ephesians 3:20–21
- ☐ Ephesians 4:2–3
- ☐ Ephesians 4:14–15
- ☐ Ephesians 2:10
- ☐ Ephesians 6:2–3

WEEK 3

- ☐ Ephesians 4:16
- ☐ Ephesians 5:8–9
- ☐ Ephesians 5:10–11
- ☐ Ephesians 4:20–24
- ☐ Ephesians 4:25–27
- ☐ Ephesians 6:11–12
- ☐ Ephesians 4:29

WEEK 4

- ☐ Ephesians 6:13–17
- ☐ Ephesians 4:31–32
- ☐ Ephesians 5:1–2
- ☐ Ephesians 6:18
- ☐ Ephesians 5:21–28
- ☐ Ephesians 5:18
- ☐ Ephesians 5:15–17

MOST POPULAR VERSES IN THE BIBLE

WEEK 1

- ☐ John 3:16
- ☐ Matthew 5:3
- ☐ Philippians 4:6–7
- ☐ Romans 12:2
- ☐ Galatians 5:22–23
- ☐ Mark 12:29–31
- ☐ Ephesians 6:12

WEEK 2

- ☐ 2 Corinthians 5:21
- ☐ Proverbs 9:10
- ☐ John 15:4
- ☐ Matthew 6:33
- ☐ 2 Corinthians 12:8–10
- ☐ Romans 11:29
- ☐ Matthew 7:7

WEEK 3

- ☐ Philippians 4:13
- ☐ 2 Timothy 3:16–17
- ☐ Matthew 5:37
- ☐ Psalm 33:15
- ☐ Proverbs 3:5–6
- ☐ John 14:26
- ☐ Romans 14:23

WEEK 4

- ☐ Psalm 46:10
- ☐ Mark 11:25
- ☐ Matthew 26:41–42
- ☐ 1 Corinthians 10:13
- ☐ 2 Timothy 1:7
- ☐ Philippians 4:8–9
- ☐ Ephesians 2:8–10

Acknowledgments

Mama: Thank you for showing me what true sacrificial love looks like. Thank you for showing me how to endure when life is hard. Thank you for being the fearless leader that you were to Jen, Allison, and me when our family fell apart. Thank you for being the glue that held us together and the glue that CONTINUES to hold us together. I wouldn't be who I am today without you, and I feel so lucky God chose you to be my mom. Thank you for always supporting my dreams, even when they didn't make sense. Thank you for raising me to love the Lord. Your faith has led me to mine, and I will always be grateful for that. I love you more than words can explain!

D bear: I knew I was the luckiest girl in the world when God blessed me with a bonus mom! Thank you for introducing me to Jesus. For not only showing me His heart but BEING His heart. You've brought me out of countless spirals, and I can genuinely say that without you I would still be crying face down on my college dorm room floor. You have been a real-life earth angel to me. Someone who ALWAYS spoke truth when I needed it and showed me TRUE unconditional love. This journal would absolutely not exist if it weren't for you. Thank you for inspiring me to be all that God has made me to be. It's because of your faith that I've gained the courage to walk mine out.

Dad: Thank you for teaching me how to love unconditionally. Thank you for teaching me that God always provides. You have NEVER stopped believing in me, and I've always felt that. Your support has kept me afloat every time I felt like I was drowning. Through every challenge, we've come out stronger, and because of that I've been able to experience God in such a REAL way. Without those tough times, I wouldn't be who I am today, and this journal and this journey would never have been born.

Jen and Allison: My sistas! Thank you for being the best sisters a girl could ask for. We have been through quite the journey together, and there is genuinely no one else I would rather go through life with. Thank you for being my biggest cheerleaders. Thank you for loving me unconditionally through every curveball decision I've made in life. You two are a part of my heart forever and have no doubt helped mold me into the person I am today. I look up to both of you more than you'll ever know. I love you so much it hurts!

Brandon and Brett: My brothas! Thank you for being the best brothers I never had! Thank you for loving my sisters so well. Thank you for always making me feel so safe to be myself. You two have healed my heart in so many ways and no doubt helped me gain the courage to keep going even when it was hard. Love you so much!

Hayden: My kiks! My bestie-pop for life. My day one. You have TRULY loved me through every season. Pre- and post-coming to know Jesus. You've seen every side of me (some no one should see lol) and have never failed to love me through them all. Your never-ending support has impacted me more than you know. You supported my dreams before they even came to life. Your words have fueled my fire on days when I felt like giving up. Your friendship helped this challenge come to life, and I will always be grateful for you!!

To all my other friends: Thank you for always encouraging me, believing in me, and praying for me! Thanks for being part of my story. Mine wouldn't be what it is without you!

To my J.E.S.U.S. Challengers: Thank you for trusting me with your heart and giving God a chance! You have changed my life in ways I'm still trying to process. Being able to lead these challenges will always be the greatest privilege of my life. I've read every little message, comment, and DM and can truly say you helped me keep going when I felt like giving up. You are my why!

MADELINE GRACE

is a young believer based in Southern California, who, while working as a social media marketer, fell in love with the possibilities for community and ministering to people through Christian TikTok. Her full-time work is the J.E.S.U.S. Challenge, which has daily posts on TikTok, Instagram, YouTube, and Facebook going through a different book of the Bible each month. She hosts the *It's Giving Grace* podcast, where she expands on topics that she believes will help people nurture their relationship with God.

CONNECT WITH MADELINE

ItsMadelineGrace.com

 @MadelineGrace   @MadelineGrace_

A Note from the Publisher

Dear Reader,

Thank you for selecting a Revell book! We're so happy to be part of your life through this work.

Revell's mission is to publish books that offer hope and help for meeting life's challenges, and that bring comfort and inspiration. We know that the right words at the right time can make all the difference; it is our goal with every title to provide just the words you need.

We believe in building lasting relationships with readers, and we'd love to get to know you better. If you have any feedback, questions, or just want to chat about your experience reading this book, please email us directly at publisher@revellbooks.com. Your insights are incredibly important to us, and it would be our pleasure to hear how we can better serve you.

We look forward to hearing from you and having the chance to enhance your experience with Revell Books.

The Publishing Team at Revell Books
A Division of Baker Publishing Group
publisher@revellbooks.com

Revell